Union and Communion

Union and Communion

THOUGHTS ON THE
SONG OF SOLOMON

by

J. HUDSON TAYLOR
Founder of the China Inland Mission

MOODY PRESS
CHICAGO

Printed in the United States of America

FOREWORD

THIS LITTLE BOOK, whose design is to lead the devout Bible student into the green pastures of the Good Shepherd, thence to the banqueting house of the King, and thence to the service of the vineyard, is one of the abiding legacies of Hudson Taylor to the church. In the power of an evident unction from the Holy One, he has been enabled herein to unfold in simplest language the deep truth of the believer's personal union with the Lord, which under symbol and imagery is the subject of the Song of Songs. And in so doing he has ministered an unfailing guidance to one of the most commonly neglected and misunderstood of the sacred Scriptures. For how many have said in bewilderment at the richness of language and profusion of figure which both conceal and reveal its meaning, "How can I understand except some man should guide me?" It is safe to say that these pages cannot fail to help and bless all such.

To those who knew him, Hudson Taylor's life was in the nature of emphasis upon the value of this small volume. For what he here expounds he also exemplified. If his words indicate the possibility and blessedness of union with Christ, his whole life declared it in actual experience. He lived as one who was "married to another, even to him who is raised from the dead," and as the outcome of that union he brought forth fruit unto God. What he *was* has given a meaning and confirmation to what he has here *said*, which cannot be exaggerated. It is inevitable that there are those who will read and reject, as mystical and unpractical, that which is so directly concerned with the intimacies of fellowship with the unseen Lord. I would, however, venture to remind such that the writer of these pages founded the China Inland Mission! He translated his vision of the Beloved into life-long strenuous service, and so kept it undimmed through all the years of a life which has had hardly a parallel in these our days.

This is really the commendation of the following short chapters. They proclaim an Evangel which has been distilled from experience, and form at least a track through this fenced portion of God's Word, which will lead many a one who treads it into the joys of Emmanuel's land.

J. STUART HOLDEN.

CONTENTS

THE SONG OF SOLOMON

INTRODUCTION

THE GREAT PURPOSE toward which all the dispensational dealings of GOD are tending is revealed to us in I Corinthians 15:28, "That God may be all in all." With this agrees the teaching of our Lord in John 17:3: "And this is [the object of] life eternal, that they might know thee the only true God, and Jesus Christ, whom thou has sent." This being so, shall we not act wisely by keeping this object ever in view in our daily life and study of God's holy Word?

All Scripture is given by inspiration of God and is profitable, and hence no part is, or can be, neglected without loss. Few portions of the

Word will help the devout student more in the pursuit of this all-important knowledge of God than the much-neglected Song of Solomon. Like other portions of the Word of God, this book has its difficulties. But so have all the works of God. Is not the fact that they surpass our unaided powers of comprehension and research a finger that points to their divine origin? Can feeble man expect to grasp divine power, or to understand and interpret the works or the providences of the All-wise? And if not, is it surprising that His Word also needs superhuman wisdom for its interpretation? Thanks be to God, the illumination of the Holy Ghost is promised to all who seek for it: what more can we desire?

Read without the key, this book is specially unintelligible, but that key is easily found in the express teachings of the New Testament. The Incarnate Word is the true key to the written Word; but even before the Incarnation, the devout student of the Old Testament would have found much help to the understanding of the sacred mysteries of this book in the prophetic writings, for there Israel was taught that her Maker was her Husband. John the Baptist, the last of the prophets, recognized the Bridegroom in the person of Christ, and said, "He that hath the bride is the bridegroom: but the friend of the bridegroom, which standeth and heareth him, rejoiceth greatly because of the bridegroom's voice: this my joy therefore is fulfilled." Paul in the fifth chapter of Ephesians goes still further, and teaches that the union of Christ with His church, and her subjection to Him, underlies the very relationship of marriage, and affords the pattern for every godly union.

In Solomon, the bridegroom king as well as author of this poem, we have a type of our Lord, the true Prince of Peace, in His coming reign. Then will be found not merely His bride, the church, but also a willing people, His subjects, over whom He shall reign gloriously. Then distant potentates will bring their wealth, and will behold the glory of the enthroned King, proving Him with hard questions, as once came the Queen of Sheba to King Solomon, and blessed will they be to whom this privilege is accorded. A brief glance will suffice them for a lifetime, but what shall be the royal dignity and blessedness of the risen and exalted bride! For ever with her Lord, for ever like her Lord, for ever conscious that His desire is toward her, she will share alike His heart and His throne. Can a study of the book which helps us to understand these mysteries of grace and love be other than most profitable?

It is interesting to notice the contrast between this book and that preceding it. The Book of Ecclesiastes teaches emphatically that "vanity of vanities, all is vanity," and is thus the necessary introduction to the Song of Solomon,

which shows how true blessing and satisfaction
are to be possessed. In like manner our Saviour's teaching in John 4 points out in a word
the powerlessness of earthly things to give lasting satisfaction, in striking contrast with the
flow of blessing that results from the presence
of the Holy Spirit—whose work it is, not to
reveal Himself but Christ as the Bridegroom of
the soul. "Whosoever drinketh of this water
shall thirst again: but whosoever drinketh of
the water that I shall give him shall never
thirst; but the water that I shall give him shall
be in him a well of water springing up [over-
flowing, on and on] unto everlasting life"
(John 4:13-14).

We shall find it helpful to consider the book
in six sections:—

I. The Unsatisfied Life and its Remedy.
1:2-2:7.

II. Communion Broken. Restoration.

2:8-3:5.

III. Unbroken Communion.

3:6-5:1.

IV. Communion again Broken. Restoration.

5:2-6:10.

V. Fruits of Recognized Union.

6:11-8:4.

VI. Unrestrained Communion.

8:5-14.

In each of these sections we shall find the speakers to be the bride, the Bridegroom, and the daughters of Jerusalem. It is not usually difficult to ascertain the speaker, though in some of the verses different conclusions have been arrived at. The bride speaks of the Bridegroom as "her Beloved," the Bridegroom speaks of her as His "love," while the address of the daughters of Jerusalem is more varied. In the first four sections they style her as the fairest among women, but in the fifth she is spoken of as the Shulamite, or the King's bride, and also as the Prince's daughter.

The student of this book will find great help in suitable Bible marking. A horizontal line marking off the address of each speaker, with a double line to divide the sections, would be useful, as also a system of vertical lines in the margin to indicate the speaker. We have ourselves ruled a single line to connect the verses which contain the utterances of the bride, a double line to indicate those of the Bridegroom, and a waved line to indicate the addresses of the daughters of Jerusalem.

It will be observed that the bride is the chief speaker in Sections One and Two, and is much occupied with herself; but in Section Three, where the communion is unbroken, she has little to say, and appears as the hearer; the daughters of Jerusalem give a long address, and the Bridegroom His longest. In that section for the first time He calls her His bride, and allures her to fellowship in service. In Section Four the bride again is the chief speaker, but after her restoration the Bridegroom speaks at length, and "upbraideth not." In Section Five, as we noticed, the bride is no longer called "the fairest among women," but claims herself to be, and is recognized as, the royal bride. In Section Six the Bridegroom claims her from her very birth, and not merely from her espousals, as God in Ezekiel 16 claimed Israel.

In the secret of His presence
   How my soul delights to hide!
Oh, how precious are the lessons
   Which I learn at Jesus' side!
Earthly cares can never vex me,
   Neither trials lay me low;
For when Satan comes to vex me,
   To the secret place I go!

THE SONG OF SOLOMON

THE TITLE

"The Song of Songs, which is Solomon's."

WELL MAY THIS BOOK be called *the* Song of
Songs! There is no song like it. Read aright, it
brings a gladness to the heart which is as far
beyond the joy of earthly things as heaven is
higher than the earth. It has been well said that
this is a song which grace alone can teach, and
experience alone can learn. Our Saviour, speaking of the union of the branch with the vine,
adds, "These things have I spoken unto you,
that my joy might remain in you, and that your
joy might be full" (John 16:11). And the
beloved disciple, writing of Him who was from

the beginning, who was with the Father, and was manifested unto us, in order that we might share the fellowship which He enjoyed, also says, "These things write we unto you, that your joy may be full." Union with Christ, and abiding in Christ—what do they not secure? Peace, perfect peace; rest, constant rest; answers to all our prayers; victory over all our foes; pure, holy living; ever-increasing fruitfulness. All, all of these are the glad outcome of abiding in Christ. To deepen this union, to make more constant this abiding, is the practical use of this precious Book.

SECTION I

Song of Solomon 1:2-2:7

THERE IS NO DIFFICULTY in recognizing the bride as the speaker in verses 2-7. The words are not those of one dead in trespasses and sins, to whom the Lord is as a root out of a dry ground—without form and comeliness. The speaker has had her eyes opened to behold His beauty, and longs for a fuller enjoyment of His love.

Let Him kiss me with the kisses of His mouth:
For Thy love [1] is better than wine.

---

[1] Loves; i.e., endearments, caresses.

21

It is well that it should be so; it marks a distinct stage in the development of the life of grace in the soul. And this recorded experience gives, as it were, a divine warrant for the desire for perceptible manifestations of His presence —perceptible communications of His love. It was not always so with her. Once she was contented in His absence—other society and other occupations sufficed her—but now it can never be so again. The world can never be to her what it once was. The betrothed bride has learned to love her Lord, and no other society than His can satisfy her. His visits may be occasional and may be brief, but they are precious times of enjoyment. Their memory is cherished in the intervals, and their repetition longed for. There is no real satisfaction in His absence, and yet, alas, He is not always with her: He comes and goes. Now her joy in Him is a heaven below, then again she is longing, and longing in vain, for His presence. Like the ever

changing tide, her experience is an ebbing and
flowing one. It may even be that unrest is the
rule, satisfaction the exception. Is there no help
for this? must it always continue so? Has He,
can He have created these unquenchable longings only to tantalize them? Strange indeed it
would be if this were the case. Yet are there
not many of the Lord's people whose habitual
experience corresponds with hers? They know
not the rest, the joy of abiding in Christ, and
they know not how to attain to it, nor why it is
not theirs. Are there not many who look back
to the delightful times of their first espousals,
who, so far from finding richer inheritance in
Christ than they then had, are even conscious
that they have lost their first love, and might
express their experience in the sad lament:

> Where is the blessedness I knew
> When first I saw the Lord?

Others, again, who may not have lost their
first love, may yet be feeling that the occasional

interruptions to communion are becoming more and more unbearable, as the world becomes less and He becomes more. His absence is an ever-increasing distress: " 'Oh that I knew where I might find him!' . . . 'Let Him kiss me with the kisses of His mouth: for thy love is better than wine.' Would that His love were strong and constant like mine, and that He never withdrew the light of His countenance!"

Poor mistaken one! There is a love far stronger than thine waiting, longing for satisfaction. The Bridegroom is waiting for thee all the time, and the conditions that debar His approach are all of thine own making. Take the right place before Him, and He will be most ready, most glad, to "satisfy thy deepest longings, to meet, supply thine every need." What should we think of a betrothed one whose conceit and self-will prevented not only the consummation of her own joy, but of his who had given her his heart? Though never at rest in his absence, she cannot trust him fully, and she does not care to give up her own name, her own rights and possessions, her own will to him who has become necessary for her happiness. She would fain claim him fully, without giving up herself fully to him. But this can never be: while she retains her own name, she can never claim his. She may not promise to love and honor if she will not also promise to obey, and until her love reaches that point of surrender she must remain an unsatisfied lover —until then she cannot, as a satisfied bride, find rest in the home of her husband. While she retains her own will and the control of her own possessions she must be content to live on her own resources—she cannot claim his.

Could there be a sadder proof of the extent and reality of the fall of man than the deep-seated distrust of our loving Lord and Master which makes us hesitate to give ourselves entirely up to Him, which fears that He might require something beyond our powers, or call for something that we should find it hard to give or to do? The real secret of an unsatisfied life lies too often in an unsurrendered will. And yet how foolish, as well as how wrong, this is! Do we fancy that we are wiser than He? or that our love for ourselves is more tender and strong than His? or that we know ourselves better than He does? How our distrust must grieve and wound afresh the tender heart of Him who was for us the Man of Sorrows! What would be the feelings of an earthly bridegroom if he discovered that his bride-elect was dreading to marry him, lest, when he had the power, he should render her life insupportable? Yet how many of the Lord's redeemed ones treat Him just so! No wonder they are neither happy nor satisfied!

But true love cannot be stationary: it must either decline or grow. Despite all the unworthy

fears of our poor hearts, divine love is destined
to conquer. The bride exclaims:

> Thine ointments have a goodly fragrance;
> Thy name is as ointment poured forth;
> Therefore do the virgins love thee.

There was no such ointment as that with
which the high priest was anointed: our Bridegroom is a priest as well as a king. The trem-
bling bride cannot wholly dismiss her fears, but
the unrest and the longing become unbearable
and she determines to surrender all, and come
what may to follow fully. She will yield her
very self to Him, heart and hand, influence and
possessions. Nothing can be so insupportable as
His absence! If He lead to another Moriah, or
even to a Calvary, she will follow Him.

> Draw me: we will run after thee!

But ah! what follows? A wondrously glad
surprise. No Moriah, no Calvary; on the con-
trary, a King! When the heart submits, then

Jesus reigns. And when Jesus reigns, there *is* rest.

And where does He lead His bride?

The King hath brought me into his chambers.

Not first to the banqueting house—that will come in due season—but first to be alone with Himself.

How perfect! Could we be satisfied to meet a beloved one only in public? No, we want to take him aside—to have him all to ourselves. So with our Master: He takes His now fully consecrated bride aside, to taste and enjoy the sacred intimacies of His wondrous love. The Bridegroom of His church longs for communion with His people more than they long for fellowship with Him, and often has to cry:

Let me see thy countenance, let me hear thy voice;
For sweet is thy voice, and thy countenance is
comely.

Are we not all too apt to seek Him because of our need rather than for His joy and pleasure? This should not be. We do not admire selfish children who only think of what they can get from their parents, and are unmindful of the pleasure that they may give or the service that they may render. But are not we in danger of forgetting that pleasing God means giving Him pleasure? Some of us look back to the time when the words "to please God" meant no more than not to sin against Him, not to grieve Him. But would the love of earthly parents be satisfied with the mere absence of disobedience? Or a bridegroom, if his bride only sought him for the supply of her own need?

A word about the morning watch may not be out of place here. There is no time so profitably spent as the early hour given to Jesus only. Do we give sufficient attention to this hour? If possible, it should be redeemed. Nothing can make up for it. We must take time to be holy!

One other thought: when we bring our questions to God, do we not sometimes either go on to offer some other petition, or leave the closet without waiting for replies? Does not this seem to show little expectation of an answer, and little desire for one? Should we like to be treated so? Quiet waiting before God would save from many a mistake and from many a sorrow.

We have found the bride making a glad discovery of a King—her King—and not a cross, as she expected. This is the first-fruit of her consecration.

> We will be glad and rejoice in thee,
> We will make mention of thy love more than of
>   wine:
> Rightly do they love thee.

Another discovery no less important awaits her. She has seen the face of the King, and, as the rising sun reveals that which was hidden in the darkness, so His light has revealed her blackness to her. "Ah," she cries, "I am black!" "But comely," interjects the Bridegroom, with inimitable grace and tenderness. "Nay, black as the tents of Kedar," she continues. "Yet to Me," He responds, "thou art comely as the curtains of Solomon!" Nothing humbles the soul like sacred and intimate communion with the Lord; yet there is a sweet joy in feeling that *He* knows *all,* and, notwithstanding, loves us still. Things once called little negligences are now seen with new eyes in the secret of His presence. There we see the mistake, the sin, of not keeping our own vineyard. This the bride confesses:

> Look not upon me, because I am swarthy,
> Because the sun hath scorched me.
> My mother's sons were incensed against me,
> They made me keeper of the vineyards;
> But mine own vineyard have I not kept.

Our attention is here drawn to a danger which is pre-eminently one of this day: the intense activity of our times may lead to zeal in service, *to the neglect of personal communion.* Such neglect will not only lessen the value

of the service, but will also tend to incapacitate
us for the highest service. If we are watchful
over the souls of others, and neglect our own
—if we are seeking to remove motes from our
brother's eye, unmindful of the beam in our
own, we shall often be disappointed with our
powerlessness to help our brethren, while our
Master will not be less disappointed in us. Let
us never forget that what we are is more important than what we do, and that all fruit
borne when not abiding in Christ must be fruit
of the flesh and not of the Spirit. As wounds
when healed often leave a scar, so the sin of
neglected communion may be forgiven and yet
the effect remain permanently.

We now come to a very sweet evidence of
the reality of the heart-union of the bride with
her Lord. She is one with the Good Shepherd:
her heart at once goes instinctively forth to the
feeding of the flock; but she would tread in the
footsteps of Him whom her soul loveth, and

would neither labor alone, nor in other companionship than His own:

> Tell me, O thou whom my soul loveth,
> Where thou feedest thy flock, where thou makest
>   it to rest at noon:
> For why should I be as one that is veiled
> Beside the flocks of thy companions?

She will not mistake the society of His servants for that of their Master.

> If thou know not, O thou fairest among women,
> Go thy way forth by the footsteps of the flock,
> And feed thy kids beside the shepherds' tents.

These are the words of the daughters of Jerusalem, and give a correct reply to her questionings. Let her show her love to her Lord by feeding His sheep, by caring for His lambs (see John 21:15-17), and she need not fear to miss His presence. While sharing with other undershepherds in caring for His flock she will find the Chief Shepherd at her side, and enjoy the tokens of His approval. It will be service *with* Jesus as well as *for* Jesus.

But far sweeter than the reply of the daughters of Jerusalem is the voice of the Bridegroom, who now speaks Himself. It is the living fruit of her heart-oneness with Him that makes His love break forth in the joyful utterances of verses 9-11. For it is not only true that our love for our Lord will show itself in feeding His sheep, but that He who when on earth said, "Inasmuch as ye have done it unto one of the least of these my brethren, ye have done it unto me," has His own heart-love stirred, and not infrequently specially reveals Himself to those who are ministering for Him.

The commendation of the bride in verse 9 is one of striking appropriateness and beauty:

I have compared thee, O my love,
To a company of horses in Pharaoh's chariots.

It will be remembered that horses originally came out of Egypt, and that the pure breed still found in Arabia was during Solomon's reign brought by his merchants for all the kings of the East. Those selected for Pharaoh's own chariot would not only be of the purest blood and perfect in proportion and symmetry, but also perfect in training, docile and obedient; they would know no will but that of the charioteer, and the only object of their existence would be to carry the king wherever he would go. So should it be with the church of Christ: one body with many members, indwelt and guided by one Spirit; holding the Head, and knowing no will but His. Her rapid and harmonious movement should cause His kingdom to progress throughout the world.

Many years ago a beloved friend, returning from the East by the overland route, made the journey from Suez to Cairo in the cumbrous stagecoach then in use. The passengers on landing took their places, about a dozen wild young horses were harnessed with ropes to the vehicle, the driver took his seat and cracked his whip, and the horses dashed off, some to the right, some to the left, and others forward, causing the coach to start with a bound, and as suddenly to stop, with the effect of first throwing those sitting in the front seat into the laps of those sitting behind, and then of reversing the operation. With the aid of sufficient Arabs running on each side to keep these wild animals progressing in the right direction the passengers were jerked and jolted, bruised and shaken, until, on reaching their destination, they were too wearied and sore to take the rest they so much needed.

Is not the church of God today more like these untrained steeds than a company of horses in Pharaoh's chariot? And while self-will and disunion are apparent in the church, can we wonder that the world still lieth in the wicked one, and that the great heathen nations are barely touched?

Changing His simile, the Bridegroom continues:

> Thy cheeks are comely with plaits of hair,
> Thy neck with strings of jewels.
> We will make thee plaits of gold
> With studs of silver.

The bride is not only beautiful and useful to her Lord, but she is also adorned, and it is His delight to add to her adornments. Nor are His gifts perishable flowers, or trinkets destitute of intrinsic value: the finest of the gold, the purest of the silver, and the most precious and lasting of the jewels are the gifts of the Royal Bridegroom to His spouse; and these, plaited into her own hair, increase His pleasure who has bestowed them.

In verses 12-14 the bride responds:

> While the King sat at his table
> My spikenard sent forth its fragrance.

It is in His presence and through His grace that whatever of fragrance or beauty may be found in us comes forth. Of Him as its source, through Him as its instrument, and to Him as its end, is all that is gracious and divine. But *He Himself* is better far than all that His grace works in us.

> My beloved is unto me as a bundle of myrrh,
> That lieth betwixt my breasts.
> My beloved is unto me as a cluster of henna-
> flowers
> In the vineyards of En-gedi.

Well is it when our eyes are filled with His beauty and our hearts are occupied with Him. In the measure in which this is true of us we shall recognize the correlative truth that His great heart is occupied with us. Note the response of the Bridegroom:

> Behold, thou art fair, my love; behold, thou art
> fair;
> Thine eyes are as dove's.

How can the Bridegroom truthfully use such words of one who recognizes herself as "black

as the tents of Kedar"? And still more strong
are the Bridegroom's words in 4:7:

> Thou art all fair, my love;
> And there is no spot in thee.

We shall find the solution of this difficulty in
II Corinthians 3. Moses in contemplation of the
Divine glory became so transformed that the
Israelites were not able to look on the glory
of his countenance. "We all, with unveiled face
[beholding and] reflecting as a mirror the glory
of the Lord, are transformed into the same
image from glory to glory [*i.e.* the brightness
caught from His glory transforms us to glory],
even as from the Lord the Spirit." Every mirror
has two surfaces. The one is dull and un-
reflecting, and is all spots; but when the reflecting surface is turned fully toward us we see
no spot, we see our own image. So while the
bride is delighting in the beauty of the Bridegroom He beholds His own image in her.
There is no spot in that: it is all fair. May we

ever present this reflection to His gaze, and to
the world in which we live for the very purpose
of reflecting Him.

Note again His words:

> Thine eyes are as dove's,

or

> Thou hast dove's eyes.

The hawk is a beautiful bird, and has beautiful
eyes, quick and penetrating; but the Bridegroom desires not hawk's eyes in His bride.
The tender eyes of the innocent dove are those
which He admires. It was as a dove that the
Holy Spirit came upon Him at His baptism,
and the dove-like character is that which He
seeks for in each of His people.

The reason why David was not permitted
to build the temple was a very significant one.
His life was far from perfect; and his mistakes
and sins have been faithfully recorded by the
Holy Spirit. They brought upon him God's
chastenings, yet it was not any of these that

disqualified him from building the temple, but rather his warlike spirit; and this though many of his battles, if not all, were for the establishment of God's Kingdom and the fulfillment of His promises to Abraham, Isaac, and Jacob. Solomon, the Prince of Peace, alone could build the temple. If we would be soul-winners and build up the church, which is His temple, let us note this: not by discussion nor by argument, but by lifting up Christ shall we draw men unto Him.

We now come to the reply of the bride. He has called her fair; wisely and well does she reply:

> Behold thou art fair, my beloved, yea, pleasant:
> Also our couch is green.
> The beams of our house are cedars,
> And our rafters are firs.
> I am [but] a rose of Sharon,
> A lily of the valleys.

The last words are often quoted as though they were the utterance of the Bridegroom, but we believe erroneously. The bride says in effect, "Thou callest me fair and pleasant, the fairness and pleasantness are Thine; I am but a wild flower, a lowly, scentless rose of Sharon (*i.e.* the autumn crocus), or a lily of the valley."

To this the Bridegroom responds: "Be it so; but if a wild flower, yet

> As a lily among thorns,
> So is my love among the daughters."

Again the bride replies:

> As the apple-tree [the citron] among the trees of
>   the wood,
> So is my beloved among the sons.
> I sat down under his shadow with great delight,
> And his fruit was sweet to my taste.

The citron is a beautiful evergreen, affording delightful shade as well as refreshing fruit. A humble wild flower herself, she recognizes her Bridegroom as a noble tree, alike ornamental and fruitful. Shade from the burning sun, refreshment and rest she finds in Him. What a contrast her present position and feelings to those with which this section commenced! He knew full well the cause of all her fears. Her distrust sprang from her ignorance of Himself, so He took her aside, and in the sweet intimacies of mutual love her fears and distrust have vanished, like the mists of the morning before the rising sun.

But now that she has learned to know Him, she has a further experience of His love. He is not ashamed to acknowledge her publicly.

> He brought me to the banqueting house,
> And his banner over me was love.

The house of wine is now as appropriate as the King's chambers were. Fearlessly and without shame she can sit at His side His acknowledged spouse, the bride of His choice. Overwhelmed with His love she exclaims:

Stay ye me with raisins, comfort me with apples:
For I am sick of love.
His left hand under my head,
And his right hand doth embrace me.

Now she finds the blessedness of being possessed. No longer her own, heart-rest is alike her right and her enjoyment; and so the Bridegroom would have it.

I adjure you, O daughters of Jerusalem,
By the roes, and by the hinds of the field,
That ye stir not up nor wake My love,
Until she [1] please.

It is never by His will that our rest in Him is disturbed.

You may always be abiding,
   If you will, at Jesus' side;
In the secret of His presence
   You may every moment hide.

---

[1] The pronoun here and in chapter 3:5, and 8:4, should not be *he* as in the King James Version, nor *it* as in the American Standard Version, but *she*.

There is no change in His Love; He is the same yesterday, today, and for ever. To us He promises, "I will never leave thee, never fail thee, nor forsake thee," and His earnest exhortation and command is, "Abide in me, and I in you."

SECTION II

Song of Solomon 2:8-3:5

"Therefore we ought to give the more earnest heed to the things that were heard, lest haply we drift away from them."—Heb. 2:1 (R.V.).

A T THE CLOSE of the first section we left the bride satisfied and at rest in the arms of her Beloved, who had charged the daughters of Jerusalem not to stir up nor awaken His love until she please. We might well suppose that a union so complete, a satisfaction so full, would never be interrupted by failure on the part of the happy bride. But alas, the experience of most of us shows how easily communion with Christ may be broken, and how needful are the exhortations of our Lord to those who are indeed branches of the true Vine, and cleansed by the Word which He has spoken, to abide in Him. The failure is never on His side. "Lo, I am with you alway." But alas, the bride often forgets the exhortation addressed to her in Psalm 45:

> Hearken, O daughter, and consider, and incline thine ear;
> Forget also thine own people, and thy father's house;
> So shall the king greatly desire thy beauty:
> For he is thy lord; and worship thou him.

In this section the bride has drifted back from her position of blessing into a state of worldliness. Perhaps the very restfulness of her new-found joy made her feel too secure. Perhaps she thought that, so far as she was concerned, there was no need for the exhortation, "Little children, keep yourselves from idols." Or she may have thought that the love of the world was so thoroughly taken away that she might safely go back, and, by a little compromise on her part, she might win her friends to follow her Lord too. Perhaps she scarcely thought at all: glad that she was saved and free, she forgot that the current—the course of this world—was against her; and insensibly glided, drifted back to that position out of which she was called, unaware all the time of backsliding. It is not necessary, when the current is against us, to turn the boat's head down the stream in order to drift, or for a runner in a race to turn back in order to miss the prize.

Ah, how often the enemy succeeds, by one device or another, in tempting the believer away from that position of entire consecration to Christ in which alone the fullness of His power and of His love can be experienced. We say the fullness of His power and of His love; for the believer may not have ceased to love his Lord.

In the passage before us the bride still loves Him truly, though not wholly. There is still a power in His Word which is not unfelt, though she no longer renders instant obedience. She little realizes how she is wronging her Lord, and how real is the wall of separation between them. To her, worldliness seems as but a little thing. She has not realized the solemn truth of many passages in the Word of God that speak in no measured terms of the folly, the danger, the sin of friendship with the world.

Love not the world, neither the things that are in the world. If any man love the world, the love of the Father is not in him.

Ye adulteresses, know ye not that the friendship of the world is enmity with God? Whosoever therefore would be a friend of the world maketh himself an enemy of God.

Be not unequally yoked with unbelievers: for what fellowship have righteousness and iniquity? or what communion hath light with darkness? And what concord hath Christ with Belial? or what portion hath a believer with an unbeliever? Wherefore

Come ye out from among them, and be ye separate, saith the Lord,

And touch no unclean thing;
And I will receive you,
And will be to you a Father,
And ye shall be to me sons and daughters, saith
  the Lord Almighty.

We have to take our choice: we cannot enjoy both the world and Christ.

The bride had not learned this: she would fain enjoy both, with no thought of their incompatibility. She observes with joy the approach of the Bridegroom.

The voice of my beloved! Behold he cometh
Leaping upon the mountains, bounding over the
  hills.
My beloved is like a gazelle or a young hart;
Behold he standeth behind our wall,
He looketh in at the windows,
He glanceth through the lattice.

The heart of the bride leaps on hearing the voice of her Beloved, as He comes in search of her. He has crossed the hills. He draws near to her. He stands behind the wall. He even looks in at the windows. With tender and touching words He woos her to come forth to Him. He utters no reproach, and His loving entreaties sink deep in her memory.

> My beloved spake, and said unto me,
> Rise up, my love, my fair one, and come away.
> For, lo, the winter is past,
> The rain is over and gone;
> The flowers appear on the earth;
> The time of the singing of birds is come,
> And the voice of the turtle is heard in our land;
> The fig-tree ripeneth her green figs,
> And the vines are in blossom,
> They give forth their fragrance.
> Arise, my love, my fair one, and come away.

All nature is responsive to the return of the summer; wilt thou, My bride, be irresponsive to My love?

Arise, my love, my fair one, and come away.

Can such pleading be in vain? Alas, it can. It was!

In yet more touching words the Bridegroom continues:

> O my dove, that art in the clefts of the rock, in the covert of the steep place,
>
> Let me see thy countenance, let me hear thy voice!
>
> For sweet is thy voice, and thy countenance is comely.

Wonderful thought, that God should desire fellowship with us, and that He whose love once made Him the Man of Sorrows may now be made the Man of Joys by the loving devotion of human hearts!

But strong as is His love, and His desire for His bride, He can come no farther. Where she now is He can never come. But surely she will go forth to Him. Has He not a claim upon her? She feels and enjoys His love; will she let His desire count for nothing? For, let us notice, it is not here the bride longing in vain for her Lord, but the Bridegroom who is seeking for her. Alas that He should seek in vain!

Take us the foxes, the little foxes, that spoil the
  vineyards;
For our vineyards are in blossom,

He continues. The enemies may be small, but
the mischief done great. A little spray of blossom, so tiny as to be scarcely perceived, is easily
spoiled, but thereby the fruitfulness of a whole
branch may be forever destroyed. And how nu-
merous the little foxes are! Little compromises
with the world, disobedience to the still small
voice in little things, little indulgences of the
flesh to the neglect of duty, little strokes of
policy, doing evil in little things that good may
come, and the beauty and the fruitfulness of the
vine are sacrificed!

We have a sad illustration of the deceitful-
ness of sin in the response of the bride. Instead
of bounding forth to meet Him, she first com-
forts her own heart by the remembrance of His
faithfulness, and of her union with Him:

My beloved is mine, and I am his:
He feedeth *his flock* among the lilies.

My position is one of security. I have no need to be concerned about it. He is mine and I am His, and nought can alter that relationship. I can find Him now at any time; He feedeth His flock among the lilies. While the sun of prosperity shines upon me I may safely enjoy myself here without Him. Should trial and darkness come He will be sure not to fail me.

Until the day be cool, and the shadows flee away,
Turn, my beloved, and be thou like a gazelle or
a young hart
Upon the mountains of Bether.

Careless of His desire, she thus lightly dismisses Him, with the thought, "A little later I may enjoy His love," and the grieved Bridegroom departs!

Poor foolish bride! She will soon find that the things that once satisfied her can satisfy no longer; and that it is easier to turn a deaf ear to

His tender call than to recall or find her absent
Lord.

The day became cool, and the shadows did
flee away, but He returned not. Then in the
solemn night she discovered her mistake: it was
dark, and she was alone. Retiring to rest she still
hoped for His return—the lesson that worldliness is an absolute bar to full communion still
unlearned.

> By night on my bed I sought him whom my soul
>   loveth:
> I sought him, but I found him not!

She waits and wearies. His absence becomes insupportable:

> *I said,* I will rise now, and go about the city,
> In the streets and in the broad ways,
> I will seek him whom my soul loveth:
> I sought him, but I found him not!

How different her position from what it might
have been! Instead of seeking Him alone, desolate and in the dark, she might have gone forth

with Him in the sunshine, leaning upon His arm. She might have exchanged the partial view of her Beloved through the lattice, when she could no longer say "Nothing between," for the joy of His embrace, and His public confession of her as His chosen bride!

> The watchmen that go about the city found me:
> *To whom I said,* Saw ye him whom my soul
>   loveth?
> It was but a little that I passed from them,
> When I found him whom my soul loveth.

She had already obeyed His command, "Arise, and come away." Fearless of reproach, she was seeking Him in the dark; and when she began to confess her Lord she soon found Him and was restored to His favor:

> I held him, and would not let him go,
> Until I had brought him into my mother's house,
> And into the chamber of her that conceived me.

Jerusalem above is the mother of us all. There

it is that communion is enjoyed, not in worldly ways or self-willed indulgence.

Communion fully restored, the section closes, as did the first, with the loving charge of the Bridegroom that none should disturb His bride:

> I adjure you, O daughters of Jerusalem,
> By the roes, and by the hinds of the field,
> [By all that is loving and beautiful and constant]
> That ye stir not up, nor awake My love,
> Until she [1] please.

May we all, while living down here, in the world, but not of it, find our home in the heavenly places to which we have been raised, and in which we are seated together with Christ. Sent into the world to witness for our Master, may we ever be strangers there, ready to confess Him the true object of our soul's devotion.

> How amiable are thy tabernacles,
> O Lord of hosts!

---

[1] See footnote on p. 44.

My soul longeth, yea even fainteth for the courts
    of the Lord;
My heart and my flesh cry out unto the living
    God.
Blessed are they that dwell in thy house:
They will be still praising thee. . . .
A day in thy courts is better than a thousand.
I had rather be a doorkeeper in the house of my
    God
Than to dwell in the tents of wickedness.
For the Lord God is a sun and shield:
The Lord will give grace and glory:
No good thing will he withhold from them that
    walk uprightly.
O Lord of hosts,
Blessed is the man that trusteth in thee.

SECTION III

THE JOY OF UNBROKEN COMMUNION

Song of Solomon 3:6-5:1

O Jesus, King most wonderful,
 Thou Conqueror renown'd,
Thou sweetness most ineffable,
 In whom all joys are found!
Thee, Jesus, may our voices bless;
 Thee may we love alone;
And ever in our lives express
 The image of Thine own.

WE HAVE BEEN mainly occupied in Sections
One and Two with the words and the experiences of the bride. In marked contrast to this,
in this section our attention is first called to the
Bridegroom, and then it is from Him that
we hear of the bride, as the object of His love

and the delight of His heart. The daughters of Jerusalem are the first speakers.

> Who is this that cometh up out of the wilderness
>   like pillars of smoke,
> Perfumed with myrrh and frankincense,
> With all powders of the merchant?

They themselves give the reply:

> King Solomon made himself a car of state
> Of the wood of Lebanon.
> He made the pillars thereof of silver,
> The bottom thereof of gold, the seat of it of
>   purple,
> The midst thereof being paved with love [love-
>   gifts],
> From the daughters of Jerusalem.
>
> Behold, it is the litter of Solomon;
> Threescore mighty men are about it,
> Of the mighty men of Israel.
> They all handle the sword, and are expert in war:
> Every man hath his sword upon his thigh,
> Because of fear in the night.

In these verses the bride is not mentioned;

she is eclipsed in the grandeur and the state of her royal Bridegroom; nevertheless, she is both enjoying and sharing it. The very air is perfumed by the smoke of the incense that ascends pillar-like to the clouds, and all that safeguards the position of the Bridegroom Himself, and shows forth His dignity, safeguards also the accompanying bride, the sharer of His glory. The car of state in which they sit is built of fragrant cedar from Lebanon, and the finest of the gold and silver have been lavished in its construction. The fragrant wood typifies the beauty of sanctified humanity, while the gold reminds us of the divine glory of our Lord, and the silver of the purity and preciousness of His redeemed and peerless church. The imperial purple with which it is lined tells us of the Gentiles—the daughter of Tyre has been there with her gift—while the love-gifts of the daughters of Jerusalem accord with the prophecy, "Even the rich among the people shall intreat thy favor."

These are the things that attract the attention of the daughters of Jerusalem, but the bride is occupied with the King Himself, and she exclaims:

Go forth, O ye daughters of Zion, and behold
    King Solomon,
With the crown wherewith his mother hath
    crowned him in the day of his espousals,
And in the day of the gladness of his heart.

The crowned King is everything to her, and she would have Him to be so to the daughters of Zion likewise. She dwells with delight on the gladness of His heart in the day of His espousals, for now she is not occupied with Him for her *own* sake, but rejoices in His joy in finding in her *His* satisfaction. Do we sufficiently cultivate this unselfish desire to be all for Jesus, and to do all for His pleasure? Or are we conscious that we principally go to Him for our own sakes, or at best for the sake of our fellow-creatures? How much of prayer there is that begins and ends with the creature, forgetful of the privilege of giving joy to the Creator! Yet it is only when He sees in our unselfish love and devotion to Him the reflection of His own that His heart can feel full satisfaction, and pour itself forth in precious utterances of love such as those which we find in the following words:

Behold, thou art fair, My love; behold, thou art fair;
Thine eyes are as dove's behind thy veil;
Thy hair is as a flock of goats,
That lie along the side of Mount Gilead;
Thy teeth are like a flock of ewes that are newly shorn,
Which are come up from the washing.
Which are all of them in pairs,
And none is bereaved among them.
Thy lips are like a thread of scarlet,
And thy speech is comely, etc. (See verses 3-5)

We have already found the explanation of the fairness of the bride in her reflecting like a mirror the beauty of the Bridegroom. Well may He with satisfaction describe her beauty while she is thus occupied with Himself! The lips that speak only of Him are like a thread of scarlet; the mouth or speech which has no word of self, or for self, is comely in His sight.

How sweet His words of appreciation and commendation were to the bride we can well imagine, but her joy was too deep for expression. She was silent in her love. She would not *now* think of sending Him away until the day be cool and the shadows flee away.

Still less does the Bridegroom think of finding His joy apart from His bride. He says:

> Until the day be cool, and the shadows flee away,
> I will get me to the mountain of myrrh,
> And to the hill of frankincense.

Separation never comes because of any withdrawing on His part. He is always ready for communion with a prepared heart, and in this happy communion the bride becomes ever fairer, and more like to her Lord. She is being progressively changed into His image, from one degree of glory to another, through the wondrous working of the Holy Spirit, until the Bridegroom can declare:

> Thou art all fair, my love;
> And there is no spot on thee.

And now she is *fit for service,* and to it the Bridegroom woos her: she will not now misrepresent Him:

> Come with me from Lebanon, my bride,
> With me from Lebanon;
> Look from the top of Amana,
> From the top of Senir and Hermon,
> From the lions' dens,
> From the mountains of the leopards

"Come with Me." It is always so. When our Saviour says, "Go ye therefore and disciple all nations," He precedes it by, "All power is given unto Me," and follows it by, "Lo, I am with you alway." Or when, as here, He calls His bride to come, it is still "with Me," and it is *in connection with this loving invitation* that for the

first time He changes the word "My love," for
the still more endearing one, "My bride."

What are lions' dens when the Lion of the
tribe of Judah is with us, or mountains of
leopards, when He is at our side! "I will fear
no evil, for thou art with me." On the other
hand, it is while His own is thus facing dangers
and toiling with Him in service, that He says:

> Thou hast ravished my heart, my sister, my bride;
> Thou hast ravished my heart with one look from
>   thine eyes,
> With one chain of thy neck.

Is it not wonderful how the heart of our Beloved can be thus ravished with the love of one
who is prepared to accept His invitation, and go
forth with Him seeking to rescue the perishing!
The marginal reading of the Revised Version is
very significant: "Thou hast ravished My heart,"
or "Thou hast given me courage." If the Bridegroom's heart may be encouraged by the fidelity
and loving companionship of his bride, it is not

surprising that we may cheer and encourage one another in our mutual service. The Apostle Paul had a steep mountain of difficulty to climb when he was being led as a captive to Rome, not knowing the things that awaited him there, but when the brethren met him at the Appii Forum he thanked God and took courage. May we ever thus strengthen one another's hands in God!

But to resume. The Bridegroom cheers the toilsome ascents and the steep pathways of danger with sweet communications of His love:

> How fair is thy love, my sister, my bride!
> How much better is thy love than wine!
> And the smell of thine ointments than all manner of spices!
> Thy lips, O my bride, drop as the honeycomb:
> Honey and milk are under thy tongue;
> And the smell of thy garments is like the smell of Lebanon.
> A garden shut up is my sister, my bride;
> A spring shut up, a fountain sealed.
> Thy shoots are a paradise of pomegranates, with precious fruits;

Henna with spikenard plants,
Spikenard and saffron,
Calamus and cinnamon, with all trees of frank-
    incense;
Myrrh and aloes, with all the chief spices.
Thou art a fountain of gardens,
A well of living waters,
And flowing streams from Lebanon.

Engaged with the Bridegroom in seeking to
rescue the perishing, the utterances of her lips
are to Him as honey and the honeycomb, and
figure is piled upon figure to express His satisfaction and joy. She is a garden full of precious
fruits and delightful perfumes, but a garden enclosed; the fruit she bears may bring blessing to
many, but the garden is for Himself alone; she
is a fountain, but a spring shut up, a fountain
sealed. And yet again she is a fountain of gardens, a well of living waters and flowing streams
from Lebanon: she carries fertility and imparts
refreshment wherever she goes; and yet it is all
of Him and for Him.

The bride now speaks for the second time in this section. As her first utterance was of Him, so now her second is for Him; self is found in neither.

> Awake, O north wind; and come, thou south;
> Blow upon my garden, that the spices thereof
>   may flow out.
> Let my beloved come into his garden,
> And eat his precious fruits.

She is ready for any experience: the north wind and the south may blow upon her garden, if only the spices thereof may flow out to regale her Lord by their fragrance. He has called her His garden, a paradise of pomegranates and precious fruits; let Him come into it and eat His precious fruits.

To this the Bridegroom replies:

> I am come into my garden, my sister, my bride:
> I have gathered my myrrh with my spice;
> I have eaten my honeycomb with my honey;
> I have drunk my wine with my milk.

Now, when she calls, He answers at once. When she is only for her Lord, He assures her that He finds all His satisfaction in her.

The section closes by the bride's invitation to His friends and hers, as well as to Himself:

> Eat, O friends;
> Drink, yea, drink abundantly, O beloved.

The consecration of all to our Master, far from lessening our power to impart, increases both our power and our joy in ministration. The five loaves and two fishes of the disciples, first given up to and blessed by the Lord, were abundant supply for the needy multitudes, and grew, in the act of distribution, into a store of which twelve hampers full of fragments remained when all were fully satisfied.

We have, then, in this beautiful section, as we have seen, a picture of unbroken communion and its delightful issues. May our lives correspond! First, one with the King, then speaking of the King; the joy of communion leading to fellowship in service, to a being all for Jesus, ready for any experience that will fit for further service, surrendering all to Him, and willing to minister all for Him. There is no room for love of the world here, for union with Christ has filled the heart. There is nothing for the gratification of the world, for all has been sealed and is kept for the Master's use.

> Jesus, my life is Thine!
> And evermore shall be
>   Hidden in Thee.
> For nothing can untwine
> Thy life from mine.

SECTION IV

COMMUNION AGAIN BROKEN—RESTORATION

Song of Solomon 5:2-6:10

THE FOURTH SECTION commences with an address of the bride to the daughters of Jerusalem, in which she narrates her recent sad experience, and entreats their help in her trouble. The presence and comfort of her Bridegroom are again lost to her, not this time by relapse into worldliness, but by slothful self-indulgence.

We are not told of the steps that led to her failure, of how self again found place in her heart. Perhaps spiritual pride in the achievements which grace enabled her to accomplish was the cause. Or, not improbably, a cherished satisfaction in the *blessing* she had received, instead of in the Blesser Himself, may have led to the separation. She seems to have been largely unconscious of her declension. Self-occupied and self-contented, she scarcely noticed His absence. She was resting, resting alone—never asking where He had gone, or how He was employed. And more than this, the door of her chamber was not only closed, but barred—an evidence that His return was neither eagerly desired nor expected.

Yet her heart was not far from Him. There was a music in His voice that awakened echoes in her soul such as no other voice could have stirred. She was still "a garden shut up, a fountain sealed" so far as the world was concerned. The snare this time was the more dangerous and insidious because it was quite unsuspected. Let us look at her narrative:

> I was asleep, but my heart waked:
> It is the voice of my beloved that knocketh
>   saying,

Open to me, my sister, my love, my dove, my
   undefiled:
For my head is filled with dew,
My locks with the drops of the night.

How often the position of the Bridegroom
is that of a knocking Suitor outside, as in His
epistle to the Laodicean [1] Church: "Behold, I
stand at the door, and knock: if any man hear
my voice, and open the door, I will come in to
him, and will sup with him, and he with me."
It is sad that He should be outside a closed door
—that He should need to knock—but still more
sad that He should knock, and knock in vain at
the door of any heart which has become His
own. In this case it is not the *position* of the
bride that is wrong. If it were, His word as before would be, "Arise, and come away";
whereas now His word is, "Open to Me, My
sister, My love." It was her *condition* of self-

---

[1] The Church of Popular Opinion, as pointed out by the
Rev. Charles Fox in an address at Keswick, as the Church
of Philadelphia is the Church of Brotherly Love.

satisfaction and love of ease that closed the door.

Very touching are His Words: "Open to Me, My sister" (He is the first-born among many brethren), "My love" (the object of My heart's devotion), "My dove" (one who has been endued with many of the gifts and graces of the Holy Spirit), "My undefiled" (washed, renewed, and cleansed for Me); and He urges her to open by reference to His own condition:

> My head is filled with dew,
> My locks with the drops of the night.

Why is it that His head is filled with the dew? Because His heart is a shepherd-heart. There are those whom the Father has given to Him who are wandering on the dark mountains of sin. Many, oh, how many, have never heard the Shepherd's voice. Many, too, who were once in the fold have wandered away—far away from its safe shelter. The heart that never can forget, the love that never can fail, *must* seek the wandering sheep until the lost one has been found. "My Father worketh hitherto, and I work." And will she, who so recently was at His side, who joyfully braved the dens of lions and the mountains of leopards, will she leave Him to seek alone the wandering and the lost?

> Open to me, my sister, my love, my dove, my
>   undefiled:
> For my head is filled with dew,
> My locks with the drops of the night.

We do not know a more touching entreaty in the Word of God, and sad indeed is the reply of the bride:

> I have put off my coat; how shall I put it on?
> I have washed my feet; how shall I defile them?

How sadly possible it is to take delight in conferences and conventions, to feast on all the good things that are brought before us, and yet to be unprepared to go out from them to self-denying efforts to rescue the perishing; to delight in the rest of faith while forgetful to fight the good fight of faith; to dwell upon the cleansing and the purity effected by faith, but to have little thought for the poor souls struggling in the mire of sin. If we can put off our coat when He would have us keep it on, if we can wash our feet while He is wandering alone upon the mountains, is there not sad want of fellowship with our Lord?

Meeting with no response from the tardy bride, her

> Beloved put in his hand by the hole of the door,
> And [her] heart was moved for him.

But, alas, the door was not only latched, but barred; and His effort to secure an entrance was in vain.

> I rose up to open to my beloved;
> And my hands dropped with myrrh,
> And my fingers with liquid myrrh,
> Upon the handles of the bolt.
> I opened to my beloved;

But my beloved had withdrawn himself, and
  was gone.
My soul had failed me when he spake.

When, all too late, the bride did arise, she
seems to have been more concerned to anoint
herself with the liquid myrrh than to speedily
welcome her waiting Lord, more occupied with
her own graces than with His desire. No words
of welcome were uttered, though her heart
failed within her, and the grieved One had
withdrawn Himself before she was ready to
receive Him. Again (as in the third chapter)
she had to go forth alone to seek her Lord, and
this time her experiences were much more painful than on the former occasion.

I sought him, but I could not find him;
I called him, but he gave me no answer.
The watchmen that go about the city found me,
They smote me, they wounded me;
The keepers of the walls took away my mantle
  from me.

Her first relapse had been one of inexperi-

ence. If a second relapse had been brought
about by inadvertence she should at least have
been ready and prompt when summoned to
obey. It is not a little thing to fall into the habit
of being tardy in obedience, even in the case of
a believer. In the case of the unbeliever the final
issue of disobedience is inexpressibly awful:

> Turn you at my reproof:
> Behold, I will pour out my Spirit unto you,
> I will make known my words unto you.
> Because I have called, and ye refused;
> I have stretched out my hand, and no man
>   regarded; . . .
> I also will laugh in the day of your
>   calamity. . . .
> Then shall they call upon me, but will I not
>   answer;
> They shall seek me diligently, but they shall not
>   find me.

The backsliding of the bride, though painful,
was not final, for it was followed by true re-
pentance. She went forth into the darkness and
sought Him. She called, but He responded not,

and the watchmen finding her, both smote and wounded her. They appear to have appreciated the gravity of her declension more correctly than she had done. Believers may be blinded to their own inconsistencies; others, however, note them, and the higher the position with regard to our Lord the more surely will any failure be visited with reproach.

Wounded, dishonored, unsuccessful in her search, and almost in despair, the bride turns to the daughters of Jerusalem and, recounting the story of her sorrows, adjures *them* to tell her Beloved that she is not unfaithful or unmindful of Him.

> I adjure you, O daughters of Jerusalem, if ye find
>   my beloved,
> That ye tell him, that I am sick of love.

The reply of the daughters of Jerusalem shows very clearly that the sorrow-stricken bride, wandering in the dark, is not recognized

as the bride of the King, though her personal
beauty does not escape notice.

> What is thy beloved more than another beloved,
> O thou fairest among women?
> What is thy beloved more than another beloved,
> That thou dost so adjure us?

This question, implying that her Beloved was
no more than any other, stirs her soul to its
deepest depths and, forgetting herself, she
pours out from the fullness of her heart a soul-
ravishing description of the glory and beauty of
her Lord.

> My beloved is white and ruddy,
> The chiefest among ten thousand.

(see verses 10-16, concluding with)

> His mouth is most sweet: yea, he is altogether
>   lovely.
> This is my beloved, and this is my friend,
> O daughters of Jerusalem.

It is interesting to compare the bride's description of the Bridegroom with the descrip-

tions of the Ancient of Days in Daniel 7:9-10, and of our risen Lord in Revelation 1:13-16. The differences are very characteristic.

In Daniel 7 we see the Ancient of Days seated on the throne of judgment. His garment was white as snow, and the hair of His head like the pure wool. His throne and His wheels were as burning fire, and a fiery stream issued and came forth from before Him. The Son of Man was brought near before Him, and received from Him dominion, and glory, and an everlasting kingdom that shall not be destroyed. In Revelation 1 we see the Son of Man Himself clothed with a garment down to the foot, and His head and His hair were white as wool, white as snow; but the bride sees her Bridegroom in all the vigor of youth, with locks "bushy, and black as a raven." The eyes of the risen Saviour are described as "a flame of fire," but His bride sees them "like doves beside the water brooks." In Revelation "His voice is as

the voice of many waters . . . and out of His
mouth proceeded a sharp two-edged sword."
To the bride, His lips are as lilies, dropping
liquid myrrh, and His mouth most sweet. The
countenance of the risen Saviour was "as the
sun shineth in his strength," and the effect of
the vision on John—"when I saw Him, I fell at
His feet as one dead"—was not unlike the effect
of the vision given to Saul as he neared Da-
mascus. But to His bride, "His aspect is like
Lebanon, excellent as the cedars." The Lion of
the tribe of Judah is to His own bride the King
of love, and, with full heart and beaming face,
she so recounts His beauties that the daughters
of Jerusalem are seized with strong desire to
seek Him with her, that they also may behold
His beauty.

> Whither is thy beloved gone,
> O thou fairest among women?
> Whither hath thy beloved turned him,
> That we may seek him with thee?

The bride replies:

My beloved is gone down to his garden, to the
   beds of spices,
To feed in the gardens, and to gather lilies.
I am my beloved's, and my beloved is mine:
He feedeth his flock among the lilies.

Forlorn and desolate as she might appear, she
still knows herself as the object of His affections, and claims Him as her own. This expression, "I am my Beloved's, and my Beloved is mine," is similar to that found in the second chapter, "My Beloved is mine, and I am His," yet with noteworthy difference. Then her first thought of Christ was of her claim upon Him: His claim upon her was secondary. Now she thinks first of His claim, and only afterward mentions her own. We see a still further development of grace in 7:10, where the bride, losing sight of her claim altogether, says:

I am my beloved's,
And his desire is toward me.

No sooner has she uttered these words and acknowledged herself as His rightful possession —a claim which she had practically repudiated when she kept Him barred out—than her Bridegroom Himself appears. And with no upbraiding word, but in tenderest love, tells her how beautiful she is in His eyes, and speaks her praise to the daughters of Jerusalem.

To her He says:

Thou art beautiful, O my love, as Tirzah,
[the beautiful city of Samaria,]
Comely as Jerusalem,
[the glorious city of the great King,]
Terrible [brilliant] as an army with banners.
Turn away thine eyes from Me,
For they have overcome Me. (See vv. 4-7.)

Then, turning to the daughters of Jerusalem, He exclaims:

There are threescore queens, and fourscore concubines,
And maidens without number.
My dove, my perfect one, is but one;

She is the only one of her mother;
She is the choice one of her that bare her.
The daughters saw her, and called her blessed;
Yea, the queens and the concubines, and they
   praised her, saying,
Who is she that looketh forth as the morning,
Fair as the moon,
Clear as the sun,
Brilliant as an army with banners?

Thus the section closes with communion fully restored, the bride reinstated and openly acknowledged by the Bridegroom as His own peerless companion and friend. The painful experience through which the bride has passed has been fraught with lasting good, and we have no further indication of interrupted communion, but in the remaining sections find only joy and fruitfulness.

SECTION V

Song of Solomon 6:11-8:4

In the second and fourth sections of this book we found the communion of the bride broken—in the former by backsliding into worldliness, and in the latter through slothful ease and self-satisfaction. The present section, like the third, is one of unbroken communion. It is opened by the words of the bride:

> I went down into the garden of nuts,
> To see the green plants of the valley,
> To see whether the vine budded.
> And the pomegranates were in flower.
> Or ever I was aware, my soul set me
> Among the chariots of my willing people.

91

As in the commencement of Section Three, the bride, in unbroken communion with her Lord, was present though unmentioned until she made her presence evident by her address to the daughters of Zion, so also in this section the presence of the King is unnoted until He Himself addresses His bride. But she is one with her Lord as she engages in His service! His promise, "Lo, I am with you alway," is ever fulfilled to her. He has no more to woo her to arise and come away, to tell her that His "head is filled with dew," His "locks with the drops of the night," or to urge her if she love Him to feed His sheep and care for His lambs. Herself His garden, she does not forget to tend it, nor keep the vineyards of others while her own is neglected. *With* Him as well as *for* Him, she goes to the garden of nuts. So thorough is the union between them that many commentators have felt difficulty in deciding whether the bride or the Bridegroom was the speaker—

and really it is a point of little moment; for, as
we have said, both were there, and of one mind,
yet we believe we are right in attributing these
words to the bride, as she is the one addressed
by the daughters of Jerusalem, and the one who
speaks to them in reply.

The bride and Bridegroom appear to have
been discovered by their willing people while
thus engaged in the happy fellowship of fruitful service, and the bride, before she was aware
of it, found herself seated among the chariots
of her people—*her* people as well as *His*.

The daughters of Jerusalem would fain call
her back:

> Return, return, O Shulammite;
> Return, return, that we may look upon thee.

There is no question now as to who she is,
nor why her Beloved is more than another beloved. He is recognized as King Solomon, and
to her is given the same name, only in its
feminine form, *Shulammite.*

Some have seen in these words, "Return, return," an indication of the rapture of the church and explain some parts of the subsequent context which appear inconsistent with this view, as resumptive rather than progressive. Interesting as is this thought, and well as it would explain the absence of *reference* to the King in the preceding verses, we are not inclined to accept it, but look on the whole song as progressive, and its last words as being equivalent to the closing words of Revelation: "Surely I come quickly. Amen. Even so, come, Lord Jesus." We do not therefore look upon the departure of the bride from her garden as being other than temporary.

The bride replies to the daughters of Jerusalem:

> Why will ye look upon the Shulammite?

or, as in the King James Version,

> What will ye see in the Shulamite?

In the presence of the King, she cannot con-
ceive why any attention should be paid to her.
As Moses, coming down from the mount, was
unconscious that his face shone with a divine
glory, so was it here with the bride. But we may
learn this very important lesson, that many who
do not see the beauty of the Lord will not fail to
admire His reflected beauty in His bride. The
eager look of the daughters of Jerusalem sur-
prised the bride, and she says, "You might be
looking upon the dance of Mahanaim [the
dance of two companies of Israel's fairest
daughters] instead of upon one who has no
claim for attention, save that she is the chosen,
though unworthy, bride of the glorious King."

The daughters of Jerusalem have no difficulty in replying to her question. Recognizing
her as of royal birth—"O Prince's daughter"—
as well as of queenly dignity, they describe in
true and Oriental language the tenfold beauties
of her person. From her feet to her head they

see only beauty and perfection. What a contrast to her state by nature! Once from the sole of the foot even unto the head was but wounds, and bruises, and festering sores; now her feet are shod with the preparation of the Gospel of peace, and the very hair of the head proclaims her a Nazarite indeed—the King Himself is held captive in the tresses thereof.

But One, more to her than the daughters of Jerusalem, responded to her unaffected question, "What will ye see in the Shulamite?" The Bridegroom Himself replies to it:

> How fair and how pleasant art thou,
> O love, for delights!

He sees in her the beauties and the fruitfulness of the tall and upright palm, of the graceful and clinging vine, of the fragrant and evergreen citron. Grace has made her like the palm tree, the emblem alike of uprightness and of fruitfulness. The fruit of the date-palm is more valued than bread by the Oriental traveler, so great is its sustaining power. The fruit-bearing powers of the tree do not pass away; as age increases the fruit becomes more perfect as well as more abundant.

> The righteous shall flourish like the palm-tree:
> He shall grow like a cedar in Lebanon.
> They that are planted in the house of the Lord
> Shall flourish in the courts of our God.
> They shall still bring forth fruit in old age;
> They shall be full of sap and green.

But why are the righteous made so upright and flourishing?

> To show that the Lord is upright;
> He is my Rock, and there is no unrighteousness
>   in Him.

One with our Lord, it is ours to *show forth* His graces and virtues, to reflect His beauty, to be His faithful witnesses.

The palm is also the emblem of victory. It raises its beautiful crown toward the heavens, fearless of the heat of the sultry sun or of the burning hot wind from the desert. From its beauty it was one of the ornaments of Solomon's, as it is to be of Ezekiel's temple. When our Saviour was received at Jerusalem as the King of Israel the people took branches of palm trees and went forth to meet Him; and in the glorious day of His espousals, a great multitude which no man can number, of all nations, and kindreds, and people, and tongues, shall stand before the throne and before the Lamb, clothed with white robes, and with palms of victory in their hands shall ascribe their salvation to our God which sitteth upon the throne, and unto the Lamb.

But if she resembles the palm she also resembles the vine. Much she needs the culture of the Husbandman, and well does she repay it. Abiding in Christ, the true source of fruitfulness, she brings forth clusters of grapes, luscious and refreshing, as well as sustaining, like the fruit of the palm—luscious and refreshing to Himself, the owner of the vineyard, as well as to the weary, thirsty world in which He has placed it.

The vine has its own suggestive lessons: it needs and seeks support; the sharp knife of the pruner often cuts away unsparingly its tender garlands and mars its appearance, while increasing its fruitfulness. It has been beautifully written:

> The living Vine, Christ chose it for Himself:—
> God gave to man for use and sustenance
> Corn, wine, and oil, and each of these is good:
> And Christ is Bread of life and Light of life.
> But yet, He did not choose the summer corn,
> That shoots up straight and free in one quick
>   growth,
> And has its day, is done, and springs no more;
> Nor yet the olive, all whose boughs are spread
> In the soft air, and never lose a leaf,
> Flowering and fruitful in perpetual peace;
> But only this, for Him and His is one—
> That everlasting, ever-quickening Vine,
> That gives the heat and passion of the world,
> Through its own life-blood, still renewed and
>   shed.

*   *   *   *   *   *

The Vine from every living limb bleeds wine;
Is it the poorer for that spirit shed?
The drunkard and the wanton drink thereof;
Are they the richer for that gift's excess?
Measure thy life by loss instead of gain;
Not by the wine drunk, but the wine poured
    forth;
For love's strength standeth in love's sacrifice;
And whoso suffers most, hath most to give.

Yet one figure more is used by the Bridegroom: "The smell of thy breath [is] like
apples [citrons]." In the first section the bride
exclaims:

As the citron-tree among the trees of the wood,
So is my beloved among the sons.
I delighted and sat down under his shadow,
And his fruit was sweet to my taste.

Here we find the outcome of that communion.
The citrons on which she had fed perfumed her
breath, and imparted to her their delicious odor.
The Bridegroom concludes his description:

Thy mouth [is] like the best wine,
That goeth down smoothly—
For my beloved—

interjects the bride,

Causing the lips of those that are asleep to move.

How wondrous the grace that has made the
bride of Christ to be all this to her Beloved!
Upright as the palm, victorious, and evermore
fruitful as she grows heavenward; gentle and
tender as the Vine, self-forgetful and self-sacri-
ficing, not merely bearing fruit in spite of ad-
versity, but bearing her richest fruits through it;
feasting on her Beloved, as she rests beneath His
shade, and thereby partaking of His fragrance
—what has grace not done for her! And what
must be her joy in finding, ever more fully, the
satisfaction of the glorious Bridegroom in the
lowly wild flower He has made His bride, and
beautified with His own graces and virtues!

I am my beloved's,
And his desire is toward me,

she gladly exclaims. Now it is none of self or for self, but all of Thee and for Thee. And if such be the sweet fruits of going down to the garden of nuts, and caring for His garden with Him, she will need no constraining to continue in this blessed service.

Come, my beloved, let us go forth into the field;
  Let us lodge in the villages.

She is not ashamed of her lowly origin, for she fears no shame. Perfect love has cast out fear. The royal state of the King, with its pomp and grandeur, may be enjoyed by and by: now, more sweet with Him at her side to make the garden fruitful; to give to Him all manner of precious fruits, new and old, which she has laid up in store for Him; and best of all to satisfy Him with her own love. Not only is she contented with this fellowship of service, but she could fain wish that there were no honors and duties to claim His attention, and for the moment to lessen the joy of His presence.

Oh that thou wert as my brother,
That sucked the breasts of my mother!
When I should find Thee without, I would kiss
  Thee;
Yea, and none would despise me.

Would that she could care for Him, and claim
His whole attention, as a sister might care for a
brother. She is deeply conscious that He has
richly endowed her, and that she is as nothing
compared with Him. But instead of proudly
dwelling upon what she has done through Him,
she would fain that it were possible for her to
be the giver and Him the receiver. Far removed
is this from the grudging thought, that must so
grate upon the heart of our Lord, "I do not
think that God requires this of me"; or, "Must
I give up that, if I am to be a Christian?" True
devotion will rather ask to be allowed to give,
and will count as loss all which may not be
given up for the Lord's sake. "I count all things
but loss, for the excellency of the knowledge of
Christ Jesus my Lord."

This longing desire to be more to Him does not, however, blind her to the consciousness that she needs His guidance, and that He is her true, her only Instructor.

> I would lead thee, and bring thee into my
>   mother's house,
> That thou mightest instruct me;
> I would cause thee to drink of spiced wine,
> Of the juice of my pomegranate.

I would give Thee my best, and yet would myself seek all my rest and satisfaction in Thee.

> His left hand should be under my head,
> And His right hand should embrace me.

And thus the section closes. There is nothing sweeter to the Bridegroom or to the bride than this hallowed and unhindered communion. And again He adjures the daughters of Jerusalem, in slightly different form:

> Why should ye stir up, or why awake my love,
> Until she [1] please?

---

[1] See footnote on p. 44.

Hallowed communion indeed! May we ever enjoy it and, abiding in Christ, we shall sing, in
the familiar words of the well-known hymn—

> Both Thine arms are clasped around me,
>   And my head is on Thy breast;
> And my weary soul hath found Thee
>   Such a perfect, perfect rest!
>   Blessed Jesus,
> Now I know that I am blest.

SECTION VI

UNRESTRAINED COMMUNION

Song of Solomon 8:5-14

W E HAVE NOW REACHED the closing section
of this book, which, as we have seen, is a poem
describing the life of a believer on earth. Beginning in Section One (1:2-2:7) with the unsatisfied longings of an espoused one—longings
which could only be met by her unreserved surrender to the Bridegroom of her soul—we find
that when the surrender was made, instead of
the cross she had so much feared she found a
King, the King of Love, who both satisfied her
deepest longings, and found His own satisfaction in her.

The second section (2:8-3:5) showed failure on her part. She was lured back again into the world, and soon found that her Beloved could not follow her there. Then, with full purpose of heart going forth to seek Him and confessing His name, her search was successful and her communion was restored.

The third section (3:6-5:1) told of unbroken communion. Abiding in Christ, she was the sharer of His security and His glory. She draws the attention, however, of the daughters of Jerusalem from these outward things to her King Himself. And, while she is thus occupied with Him, and would have others so occupied, she finds that her royal Bridegroom is delighting in her and inviting her to fellowship of service, fearless of dens of lions and mountains of leopards.

The fourth section (5:2-6:10), however, shows again failure; not as before through worldliness, but rather through spiritual pride and sloth. Restoration now was much more difficult, but again when she went forth diligently to seek her Lord and so confessed Him as to lead others to long to find Him with her, He revealed Himself and the communion was restored, to be interrupted no more.

The fifth section (6:11-8:4), as we have seen, describes not only the mutual satisfaction and delight of the bride and Bridegroom in each other, but the recognition of her position and her beauty by the daughters of Jerusalem.

And now in the sixth section (8:5-14) we come to the closing scene of the book. In it the bride is seen leaning upon her Beloved, asking Him to bind her yet more firmly to Himself, and occupying herself in His vineyard, until He calls her away from earthly service. To this last section we shall now give our attention more particularly.

It opens, as did the third, by an inquiry or exclamation of the daughters of Jerusalem.

There they asked, "Who is this that cometh out
of the wilderness like pillars of smoke, *etc.?*"
but then their attention was claimed by the
pomp and state of the King, not by His person,
nor by that of His bride. Here they are attracted
by the happy position of the bride in relation to
her Beloved, and not by their surroundings.

> Who is this that cometh up from the wilderness,
> Leaning upon her beloved?

It is through the bride that attention is drawn
to the Bridegroom; their union and communion
are now open and manifest. For the last time
the wilderness is mentioned; but sweetly solaced
by the presence of the Bridegroom, it is *no
wilderness to the bride.* In all the trustfulness of
confiding love she is seen leaning upon her
Beloved. He is her strength, her joy, her pride,
and her prize, while she is His peculiar treasure,
the object of His tenderest care. All His resources of wisdom and might are hers; though
journeying she is at rest, though in the wilder-

ness she is satisfied, while leaning upon her Beloved.

Wonderful, however, as are the revelations of grace and love to the heart taught by the Holy Spirit through the relationship of bride and Bridegroom, the Christ of God is more than Bridegroom to His people. He who when on earth was able to say, "Before Abraham was, I am," here claims His bride from her very birth, and not alone from her espousals. Before she knew Him, He knew her, and of this He reminds her in the words:

> I raised thee up under the citron-tree;
> There thy mother brought thee forth.

He takes delight in her beauty, but that is not so much the cause as the effect of His love, for He took her up when she had no comeliness. The love that has made her what she is, and now takes delight in her, is not a fickle love, nor need she fear its change.

Gladly does the bride recognize this truth, that she is indeed His own, and she exclaims:

> Set me as a seal upon thine heart, as a seal upon thine arm:
> For love is strong as death;
> Jealousy [ardent love] is cruel [retentive] as the grave;
> The flashes thereof are flashes of fire,
> A very flame of the Lord.

The High Priest bore the names of the twelve tribes upon his heart, each name being engraved as a seal in the costly and imperishable stone chosen by God, each seal or stone being set in the purest gold; he likewise bore the same names upon his shoulders, indicating that both the love and the strength of the High Priest were pledged on behalf of the tribes of Israel. The bride would be thus upborne by Him who is alike her Prophet, Priest, and King, for love is strong as death, and jealousy, or ardent love, retentive as the grave. Not that she doubts the constancy of her Beloved, but that she has learned, alas, the inconstancy of her own heart, and she would be bound to the heart and arm of her Beloved as with chains and settings of gold, even the emblem of deity. Thus the Psalmist prayed, "Bind the sacrifice with cords, even unto the horns of the altar."

It is comparatively easy to lay the sacrifice on the altar that sanctifies the gift, but it requires divine compulsion—the cords of love—to retain it there. So here the bride would be set and fixed on the heart and on the arm of Him who is henceforth to be her all in all, that she may evermore trust only in that love, be sustained only by that power.

Do we not all need to learn a lesson from this? and to pray to be kept from turning to Egypt for help, from trusting in horses and chariots, from putting confidence in princes, or in the son of man, rather than in the living God? How the kings of Israel, who had won great triumphs by faith, sometimes turned aside

to heathen nations in their later years! The Lord
keep His people from this snare.

The bride continues: "The flashes of love are
flashes of fire, a very flame of the Lord." It is
worthy of note that this is the only occurrence
of this word, "Lord" in this book. But how
could it be omitted here? For love is of God,
and God is love.

To her request the Bridegroom replies with
reassuring words:

> Many waters cannot quench love,
> Neither can the floods drown it:
> If a man would give all the substance of his
>   house for love,
> It would utterly be contemned.

The love which grace has begotten in the
heart of the bride is itself divine and persistent;
many waters cannot quench it, nor the floods
drown it. Suffering and pain, bereavement and
loss may test its constancy, but they will not
quench it. Its source is not human or natural.
Like the life, it is hidden with Christ in God.

What "shall separate us from the love of Christ? shall tribulation, or distress, or persecution, or famine, or nakedness, or peril, or sword? . . . Nay, in all these things we are more than conquerors through Him that loved us. For I am persuaded that neither death, nor life, nor angels, nor principalities, nor powers, nor things present, nor things to come, nor height, nor depth, nor any other creation [A.R.V. margin], shall be able to separate us from the love of God, which is in Christ Jesus our Lord." Our love to God is secured by God's love to us. To the soul really rescued by grace, no bribe to forsake God's love will be finally successful. "If a man would give all the substance of his house for love, it would utterly be contemned."

Freed from anxiety on her own account, the happy bride next asks guidance, and fellowship in service with her Lord, on behalf of those who have not yet reached her favored position.

We have a little sister,
And she hath no breasts:
What shall we do for our sister
In the day when she shall be spoken for?

How beautifully her conscious union with the Bridegroom appears in her expressions. "*We* have a little sister," not *I* have, etc.; "what shall *we* do for our sister," etc.? She has neither private relationships nor interests; in all things she is one with Him. And we see a further development of grace in the very question. Toward the close of the last section she recognized the Bridegroom as her Instructor. She will not now make her own plans about her little sister, and ask His acquiescence in them. She will rather learn what His thoughts are, and have fellowship with Him in His plans.

How much anxiety and care the children of God would be spared if they learned to act in this way! Is it not too common to make the best plans that we can, and to carry them out as best we may, feeling all the while a great burden of responsibility, and earnestly asking the Lord to help *us?* Whereas if we always let *Him* be our Instructor in service, and leave the responsibility with *Him,* our strength would not be exhausted with worry and anxiety, but all would be at His disposal, and accomplish His ends.

In the little sister, as yet immature, may we not see the elect of God, given to Christ in God's purpose, but not yet brought into saving relation to Him? And perhaps also those babes in Christ who as yet need feeding with milk and not with meat, but who, with such care, will in due time become experienced believers, fitted for the service of the Lord? Then they will be spoken for, and called into that department of service for which He has prepared them.

The Bridegroom replies:

If she be a wall,
We will build upon her battlements of silver;
And if she be a door,
We will inclose her with boards of cedar.

In this reply the Bridegroom sweetly recognizes His oneness with His bride, in the same way as she has shown her conscious oneness with Him. As she says, "What shall *we* do for our sister?" so He replies, *"We* will build . . . *we* will inclose," etc. He will not carry out His purposes of grace irrespective of His bride, but will work with and through her. What can be done for this sister, however, will depend upon what she becomes. If she be a wall, built upon the true foundation, strong and stable, she shall be adorned and beautified with battlements of silver. But if unstable and easily moved to and fro like a door, such treatment will be as impossible as unsuitable—she will need to be enclosed with boards of cedar, hedged in with restraints for her own protection.

The bride rejoicingly responds, "I am a wall." She knows the foundation on which she is built. There is no *if* in her case. She is conscious of having found favor in the eyes of her

Beloved. Naphtali's blessing is hers: she is "satisfied with favor, and full with the blessing of the Lord."

But what is taught by the connection of this happy consciousness with the lines which follow?

Solomon had a vineyard at Baal-hamon;
He let out the vineyard unto keepers;
Every one for the fruit thereof was to bring a
    thousand pieces of silver.
My vineyard, which is mine, is before me:
Thou, O Solomon, shalt have the thousand,
And those that keep the fruit thereof two hun-
    dred.

The connection is, we believe, one of great importance, teaching us that what she *was* (by grace) was more important than what she *did,* and that she did not work in order to earn favor, but being assured of favor, gave her love free scope to show itself in service. The bride knew her relationship to her Lord, and His love to her. And in her determination that

He should have the thousand pieces of silver, her concern was that her vineyard should not produce less for her Solomon than His vineyard at Baal-hamon. Her vineyard was herself, and she desired for her Lord much fruit. She would see too that the keepers of the vineyard, those who were her companions in its culture, and who ministered in word and doctrine, were well rewarded. She would not muzzle the ox that treadeth out the corn. A full tithe, nay a double tithe, was to be the portion of those who kept the fruit and labored with her in the vineyard.

How long this happy service continues, and how soon it is to be terminated, we cannot tell. He who calls His servants to dwell in the gardens, and cultivate them for Him—as Adam of old was placed in the Paradise of God—it is He alone who knows the limit of this service. Sooner or later the rest will come, the burden and heat of the last day will have been borne,

the last conflict will be over, and the voice of
the Bridegroom will be heard addressing His
loved one:

> Thou that dwellest in the gardens,
> The companions hearken to thy voice:
> Cause me to hear it.

Thy service among the companions is finished. Thou hast fought the good fight, thou
hast kept the faith, thou hast finished thy
course; henceforth there is laid up for thee the
crown of righteousness, and the Bridegroom
Himself shall be thine exceeding great reward!

Well may the bride let Him hear her voice,
and, springing forth in heart to meet Him,
cry:

> Make haste, my beloved,
> And be thou like to a roe or to a young hart
> Upon the mountains of spices!

She no longer asks Him, as in the second section:

Turn, my beloved, and be thou like a roe or a
   young hart
Upon the mountains of Bether [separation].

She has never again wished Him to turn away
from her, for there are no mountains of Bether
to those who are abiding in Christ; now there
are mountains of spices. He who inhabits the
praises of Israel, which rise like the incense of
spices from His people's hearts, is invited by
His bride to make haste, to come quickly, and
be like a roe or young hart upon the mountains
of spices.

Very sweet is the presence of our Lord, as by
His Spirit He dwells among His people, while
they serve Him below. But here there are many
thorns in every path, which call for watchful
care, and it is meet that now we should suffer
with our Lord in order that we may hereafter
be glorified together. The day is soon coming,
however, in which He will bring us up out of
the earthly gardens and associations to the

palace of the great King. There His people "shall hunger no more, neither thirst any more; neither shall the sun light on them, nor any heat. For the Lamb, which is in the midst of the throne, shall feed them, and shall lead them unto living fountains of waters; and God shall wipe away all tears from their eyes."

> The Spirit and the bride say, Come! . . .
> Surely I come quickly.
> Amen; even so, come, Lord Jesus!

APPENDIX

THE DAUGHTERS OF JERUSALEM

THE QUESTION is frequently asked, Who are represented by the daughters of Jerusalem?

They are clearly not the bride, yet they are not far removed from her. They know where the Bridegroom makes His flock to rest at noon; they are charged by the Bridegroom not to stir up nor awaken His love when she rests, abiding in Him. They draw attention to the Bridegroom as with dignity and pomp He comes up from the wilderness. Their love-gifts adorn His chariot of state. They are appealed to by the bride for help in finding her Beloved and, stirred by her impassioned description of His beauty, they desire to seek Him with her. They describe very fully the beauty of the bride, but on the other hand we never find them occupied with the *person* of the Bridegroom; *He* is not all in all to them; they mind outward and earthly things.

Do they not represent those who are for the present more concerned about the things of this world than the things of God? To advance their own interests and to secure their own comfort concerns them more than to be in all things pleasing to the Lord. They *may* form part of that great company spoken of in Rev. 7:9-17, who come out of the great tribulation, but they will not form part of the 144,000, "the first-fruits unto God and to the Lamb" (Rev. 14:1-5). They have forgotten the warning of our Lord in Luke 21:34-36, and hence they are not "accounted worthy to escape all these things that shall come to pass, and to stand before the Son of Man." They have not, with Paul, counted "all things but loss for the excellency of the knowledge of Christ Jesus the Lord."

We wish to place on record our solemn conviction that not all who are called Christians, or think themselves to be such, will attain to that resurrection of which St. Paul speaks in Phil. 3:11, or will thus meet the Lord in the air. Unto those who by lives of consecration manifest that they are not of the world, but are looking for Him, He will appear without sin unto salvation.